Entry to English Literacy

A Real-Life Approach

Author

Kathleen Kelley Beal

Reviewers

Beth Powell
Literacy Specialist
Houston Community College

Kathleen Santopietro
Consultant, Adult Basic Education
Colorado Department of Education

STECK-VAUGHN
C O M P A N Y
A Subsidiary of National Education Corporation

Acknowledgments

About the Author

Kathleen Kelley Beal is an experienced educator in the field of English as a Second Language. She has taught ESL at the University of Colorado, in Boulder, Colorado, at Fort Steilacoom Community College in Tacoma, Washington, and at Mott Community College in Flint, Michigan. She has served as consultant and presenter at many ESL workshops and conferences and is the author of *Speaking of Pictures,* a conversation-oriented program for adult ESL students.

Photography

Cover: Crowd, © Paul Henning/UNIPHOTO; Street, © Richard Laird/FPG
Inside Photography:
    Stan Kearl (p. 50)

Illustration

Linda Butler
Sue Durban

Staff Credits

Supervising Editor: Carolyn M. Hall
Senior Editor: Beverly A. Grossman
Cover Design: Joyce Spicer

ISBN 0-8114-4635-2

Contents

Aa	(A)rgentin(a)	any	Africa
	America	are	make
	Alaska	Saudi Arabia	army
Bb	Brazil	big	back
	able	Baltimore	Burma
	about	Boston	cable
Cc	can	China	Cuba
	Costa Rica	Canada	Cambodia
	car	California	march
Dd	Dayna	Detroit	good
	do	did	Dallas
	December	Dwight	done
Ee	Ethiopia	end	Easter
	made	England	even
	Egypt	each	eager
Ff	far	France	Florida
	life	first	for
	San Francisco	Friday	leaf
Gg	Greece	again	group
	going	Georgia	Germany
	get	Gary	began

Hh	Haiti Hawaii such	she holiday had	hand Hong Kong hollow
Ii	in Indian Iran	like if find	Indonesia Illinois insect
Jj	judge Judy just	join Japan Juan	June job jury
Kk	Kelley Kenya Korea	make know kind	Kuwait take blink
Ll	Libya all last	Louisiana look Laos	Los Angeles let tile
Mm	Monday number Meng	Mexico Minneapolis moon	name mom money
Nn	November Neng Nicaragua	any next Navajo	long never ant

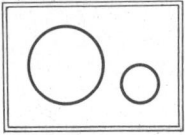

Oo	Ohio got Olga	Oregon of on	do October only
Pp	Poland Philippines Pacific	help place Philip	open put popular
Qq	Quebec quarter quick	Queen quiet Quito	Quincy question quill
Rr	right Russia river	room Ricardo Rhodesia	your work silver
Ss	Sweden Siang so	must South America is	Spanish saw sing
Tt	Taiwan into take	Tennessee Thailand out	the Tien total
Uu	Utah use Uruguay	put United States nut	you rural Europe

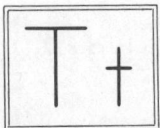

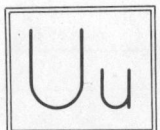

V v	Vermont	every	Vietnam
	Venezuela	vegetable	very
	even	Vang	vain

W w	Washington	when	water
	was	Wendy	West Virginia
	what	Wednesday	windy

X x	Xavier	box	ax
	oxen	X-ray	tax
	Xenia	Xanthus	extra

Y y	Yang	Yugoslavia	your
	Yemen	York	fly
	yet	year	toy

Z z	Zurich	zone	Zamora
	dozen	zipper	Zaire
	zero	Zambia	lazy

D d Did Dayna and Dwight get back in October?

E e Easter is celebrated in England and France.

M m Next Monday Neng will get a new number.

4

also	h	y	a	p	l	t	s	h	o
like	a	l	z	i	u	k	e	j	m
they	t	s	h	q	e	y	n	v	d
Laos	L	F	p	a	c	o	v	s	e
very	v	o	e	q	r	d	g	f	y
with	w	u	i	l	t	m	r	x	h
FIRE	T	F	L	I	H	R	B	E	D
face	f	l	a	r	c	a	e	h	n
EXIT	E	F	S	J	X	I	L	T	D
OPEN	D	O	P	D	E	F	M	N	M
WORK	W	V	M	O	C	R	N	H	K
NAME	N	M	H	A	N	M	N	F	E

also	alos	aols	also	aslo
like	liek	like	ilke	elik
they	they	tehy	hyte	ythe
Laos	Loas	Lsoa	Laos	Lsao
very	vrey	vyre	veyr	very
with	wthi	thiw	wiht	with
FIRE	ERIF	FIRE	FRIE	RFEI
face	face	fcea	feca	faec
EXIT	ETIX	XETI	EXIT	ITEX
OPEN	PENO	OPEN	OEPN	NOPE
work	wrok	wkro	work	rowk
name	nmae	mane	nema	name

| **Aa** | Laotian | airplane | Saudi Arabia |
| | Spanish | call | Alan |

| **Ee** | Sweden | Persia | teacher |
| | jet | Egypt | English |

| **Ii** | Indian | pill | Thai |
| | write | Italian | Vietnamese |

| **Oo** | Oliver | open | front |
| | out | Korean | Pacific Ocean |

| **Uu** | duck | Uganda | University of Utah |
| | hunt | rug | use |

| **Gg** | Craig told George to be quiet. |

1. train	h	t	y	r	l	a	i	m	n
2. French	E	F	c	r	e	b	n	c	h
3. BUS	D	P	B	R	U	O	Z	S	J

1. mail	mali	mail	amil	lmai
2. STOP	POST	TSOP	STPO	STOP
3. RIVER	RIVRE	RIVER	RVIER	RIVRE

Aa Bb Cc Dd Ee Ff Gg Hh Ii
Jj Kk Ll Mm Nn Oo Pp Qq Rr
Ss Tt Uu Vv Ww Xx Yy Zz

money

man

mop

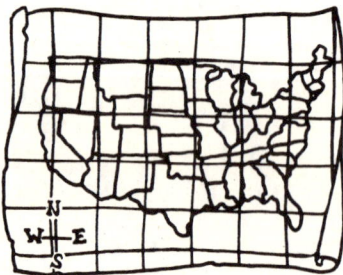
map

milk

moon

1. Mm   2. Mm   3. Mm

4. Mm   5. Mm   6. Mm

7. Mm   8. Mm   9. Mm

Aa Bb Cc Dd Ee Ff Gg Hh Ii
Jj Kk Ll Mm Nn Oo Pp Qq Rr
Ss Tt Uu Vv Ww Xx Yy Zz

sun

snow

stamp

soap

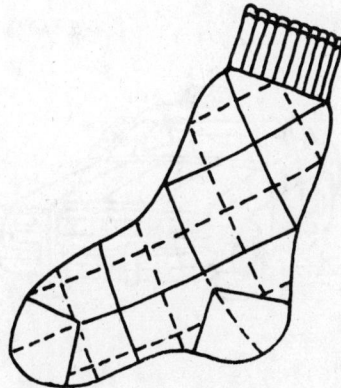

sock

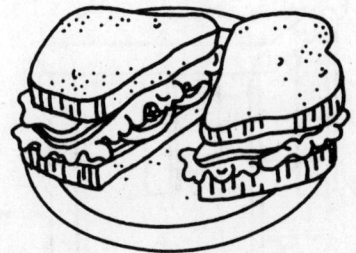

sandwich

1. Ss
2. Ss
3. Ss

4. Ss
5. Ss
6. Ss

7. Ss
8. Ss
9. Ss

Aa Bb Cc Dd Ee Ff Gg Hh Ii Jj Kk Ll Mm Nn Oo Pp Qq Rr Ss [Tt] Uu Vv Ww Xx Yy Zz

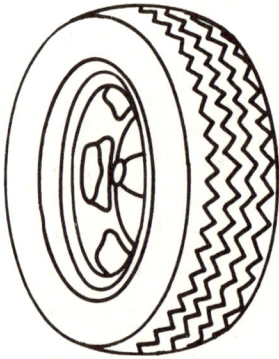

tire

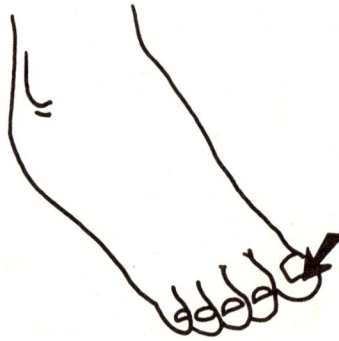

toe

tape

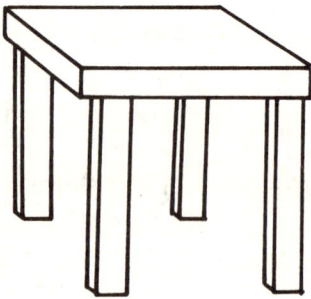

table

taxi

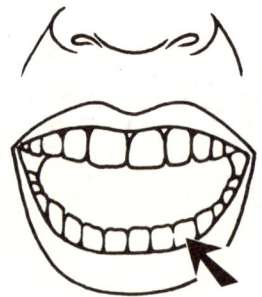

teeth

1. Tt   2. Tt   3. Tt

4. Tt   5. Tt   6. Tt

7. Tt   8. Tt   9. Tt

Aa Bb Cc Dd Ee Ff Gg Hh Ii
Jj Kk Ll Mm Nn Oo Pp Qq Rr
Ss Tt Uu Vv Ww Xx Yy Zz

pencil

purse

pan

piano

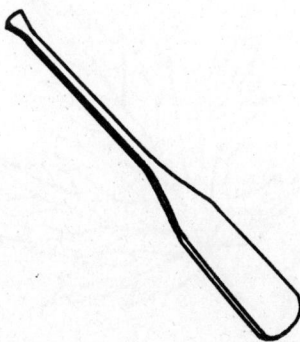

paddle

pot

1. Pp   2. Pp   3. Pp

4. Pp   5. Pp   6. Pp

7. Pp   8. Pp   9. Pp

Aa Bb Cc Dd Ee Ff Gg Hh Ii
Jj Kk Ll Mm Nn Oo Pp Qq Rr
Ss Tt Uu Vv Ww Xx Yy Zz

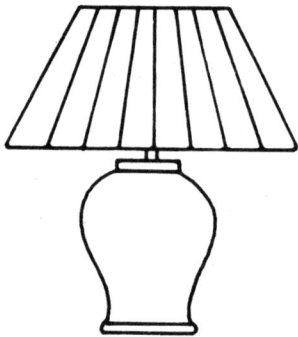

lamp

ladder

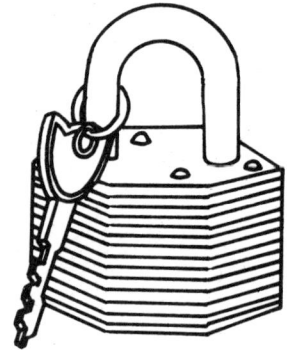

lock

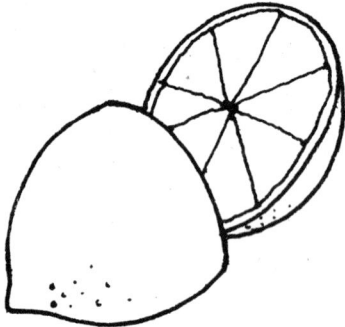

lemon

leaf

lizard

1. Ll   2. Ll   3. Ll

4. Ll   5. Ll   6. Ll

7. Ll   8. Ll   9. Ll

Aa Bb Cc Dd Ee Ff Gg Hh Ii
Jj Kk Ll Mm Nn Oo Pp Qq Rr
Ss Tt Uu Vv Ww Xx Yy Zz

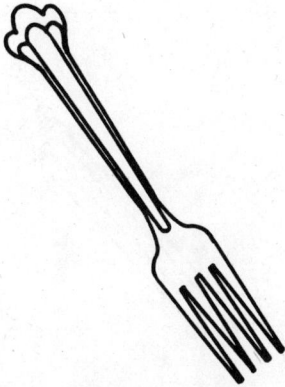

fork

fire

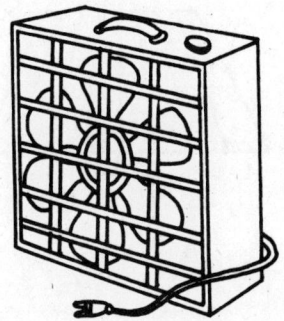

fan

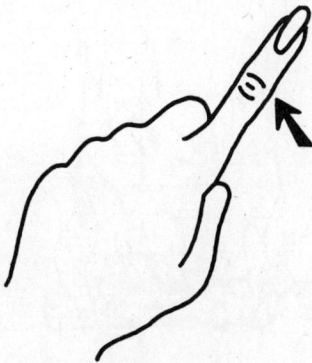

finger

fish

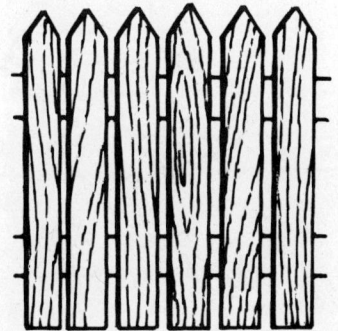

fence

1. Ff   2. Ff   3. Ff

4. Ff   5. Ff   6. Ff

7. Ff   8. Ff   9. Ff

_____ish

_____oap

_____ilk

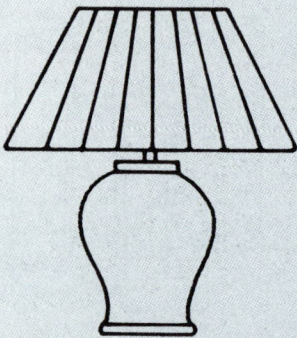

_____amp

_____able

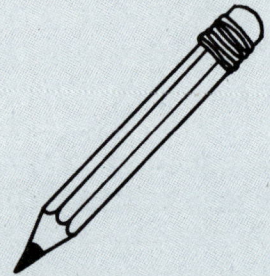

_____encil

_____oney

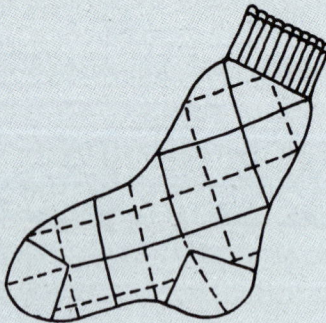

_____ock

_____ire

1. _____

2. _____

3. _____

4. _____

5. _____

6. _____

7. _____

8. _____

9. _____

Aa Bb Cc Dd Ee Ff Gg Hh Ii
Jj Kk Ll Mm Nn Oo Pp Qq Rr
Ss Tt Uu Vv Ww Xx Yy Zz

belt

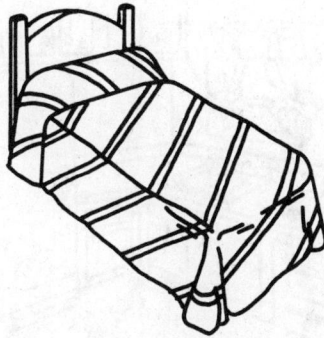

bed

bench

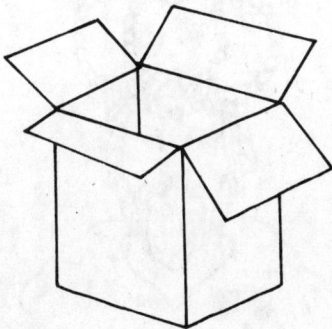

box

bus

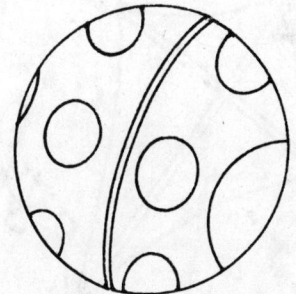

ball

1. Bb   2. Bb   3. Bb

4. Bb   5. Bb   6. Bb

7. Bb   8. Bb   9. Bb

Aa Bb Cc Dd Ee Ff Gg Hh Ii
Jj Kk Ll Mm Nn Oo Pp Qq Rr
Ss Tt Uu Vv Ww Xx Yy Zz

key

kitchen

kitten

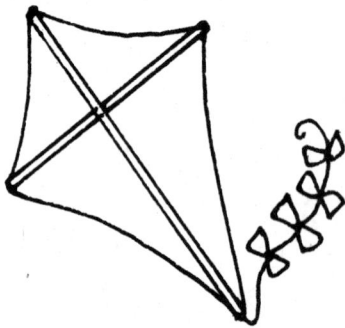
kite

kettle

king

1. Kk   2. Kk   3. Kk

4. Kk   5. Kk   6. Kk

7. Kk   8. Kk   9. Kk

Aa Bb Cc Dd Ee Ff Gg Hh Ii
Jj Kk Ll Mm Nn Oo Pp Qq Rr
Ss Tt Uu Vv Ww Xx Yy Zz

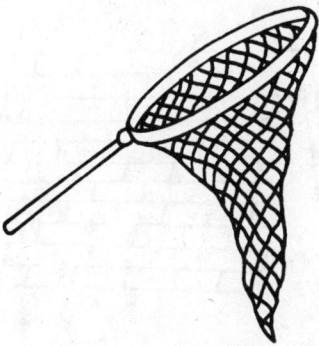

net

newspaper

nickel

nest

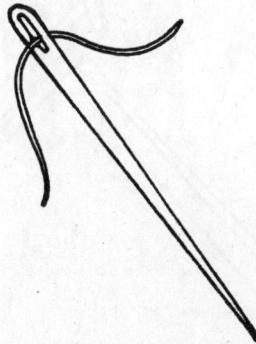

needle

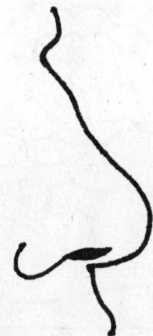

nose

1. Nn   2. Nn   3. Nn

4. Nn   5. Nn   6. Nn

7. Nn   8. Nn   9. Nn

Aa Bb Cc Dd Ee Ff Gg Hh Ii
Jj Kk Ll Mm Nn Oo Pp Qq [Rr]
Ss Tt Uu Vv Ww Xx Yy Zz

radio

rug

roof

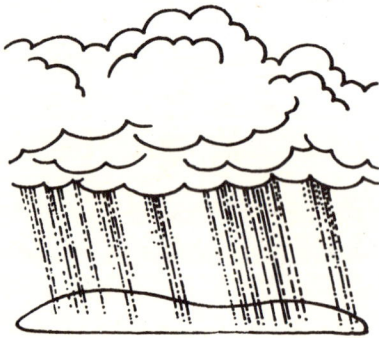

rain

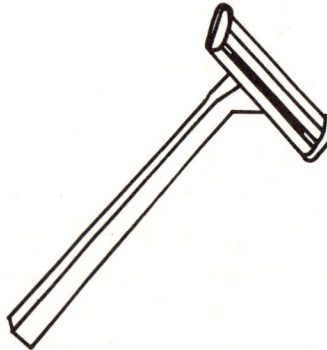

razor

record

1. Rr   2. Rr   3. Rr

4. Rr   5. Rr   6. Rr

7. Rr   8. Rr   9. Rr

Aa Bb Cc |Dd| Ee Ff Gg Hh Ii
Jj Kk Ll Mm Nn Oo Pp Qq Rr
Ss Tt Uu Vv Ww Xx Yy Zz

dog

door

dress

doctor

desk

dollar

1. Dd   2. Dd   3. Dd

4. Dd   5. Dd   6. Dd

7. Dd   8. Dd   9. Dd

Aa Bb Cc Dd Ee Ff Gg Hh Ii
Jj Kk Ll Mm Nn Oo Pp Qq Rr
Ss Tt Uu Vv Ww Xx Yy Zz

zebra

zoo

zero

Zip Code

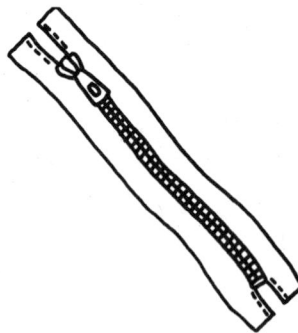

zipper

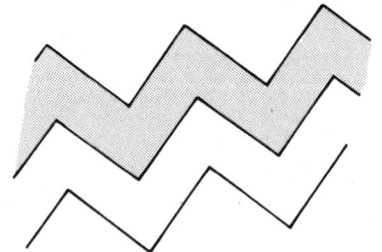

zig zag

1. Zz 2. Zz 3. Zz

4. Zz 5. Zz 6. Zz

7. Zz 8. Zz 9. Zz

____ey

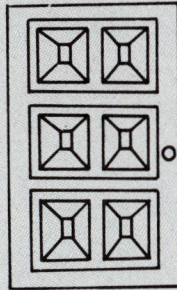

____oor

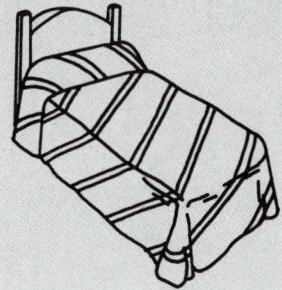

____ed

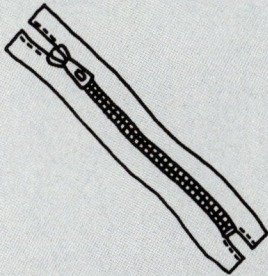

____ipper

____ain

____ickel

____us

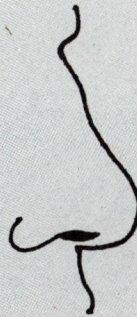

____ose

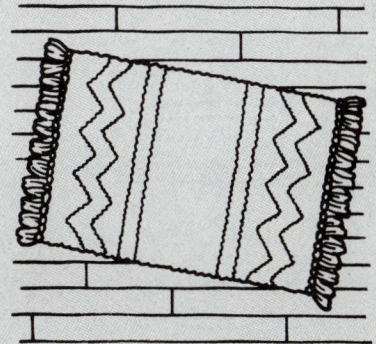

____ug

1. _____

2. _____

3. _____

4. _____

5. _____

6. _____

7. _____

8. _____

9. _____

Aa Bb Cc Dd Ee Ff Gg Hh Ii
Jj Kk Ll Mm Nn Oo Pp Qq Rr
Ss Tt Uu Vv Ww Xx Yy Zz

coat

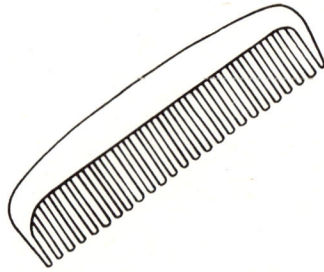

comb

cat

cup

car

can

1. Cc   2. Cc   3. Cc

4. Cc   5. Cc   6. Cc

7. Cc   8. Cc   9. Cc

Aa Bb Cc Dd Ee Ff Gg **Hh** Ii
Jj Kk Ll Mm Nn Oo Pp Qq Rr
Ss Tt Uu Vv Ww Xx Yy Zz

hat

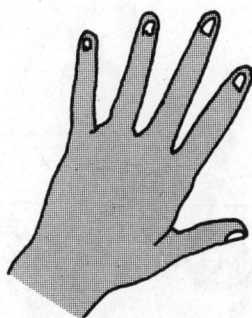

hand

house

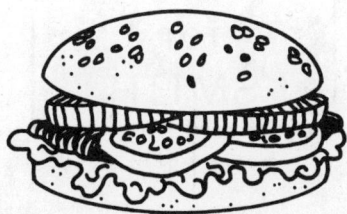

hamburger

hose

horse

1. Hh   2. Hh   3. Hh

4. Hh   5. Hh   6. Hh

7. Hh   8. Hh   9. Hh

Aa Bb Cc Dd Ee Ff Gg Hh Ii
Jj Kk Ll Mm Nn Oo Pp Qq Rr
Ss Tt Uu |Vv| Ww Xx Yy Zz

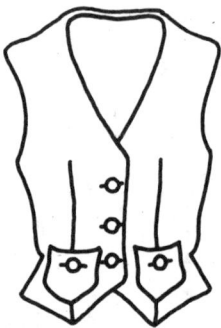

vest

van

vase

violin

vegetables

vote

1. Vv   2. Vv   3. Vv

4. Vv   5. Vv   6. Vv

7. Vv   8. Vv   9. Vv

Aa Bb Cc Dd Ee Ff Gg Hh Ii
Jj Kk Ll Mm Nn Oo Pp Qq Rr
Ss Tt Uu Vv Ww Xx Yy Zz

jar

jacket

jeep

judge

jump

jet

1. Jj   2. Jj   3. Jj

4. Jj   5. Jj   6. Jj

7. Jj   8. Jj   9. Jj

Aa Bb Cc Dd Ee Ff Gg Hh Ii
Jj Kk Ll Mm Nn Oo Pp Qq Rr
Ss Tt Uu Vv Ww Xx Yy Zz

gas

gift

glass

grapes

gum

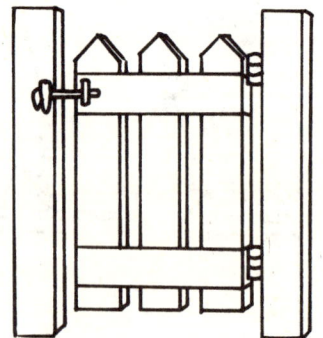

gate

1. Gg   2. Gg   3. Gg

4. Gg   5. Gg   6. Gg

7. Gg   8. Gg   9. Gg

Aa Bb Cc Dd Ee Ff Gg Hh Ii
Jj Kk Ll Mm Nn Oo Pp Qq Rr
Ss Tt Uu Vv [Ww] Xx Yy Zz

window

well

wave

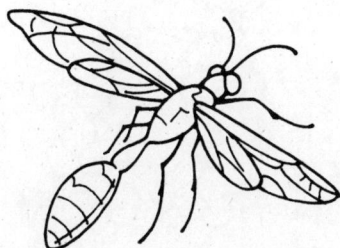

wasp

wood

watch

1. Ww   2. Ww   3. Ww

4. Ww   5. Ww   6. Ww

7. Ww   8. Ww   9. Ww

_____ar

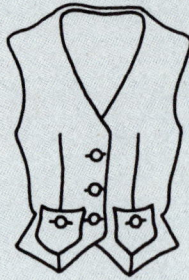

_____est

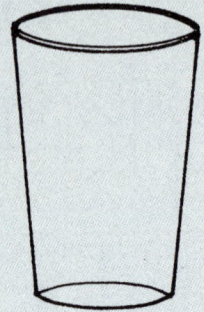

_____lass

_____indow

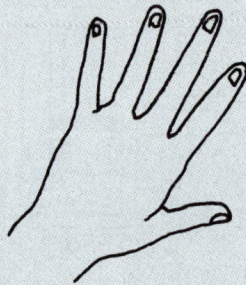

_____and

_____ump

_____up

_____at

_____rapes

1. _____   2. _____   3. _____

4. _____   5. _____   6. _____

7. _____   8. _____   9. _____

Aa Bb Cc Dd Ee Ff Gg Hh Ii
Jj Kk Ll Mm Nn Oo Pp Qq Rr
Ss Tt Uu Vv Ww Xx [Yy] Zz

yard

yarn

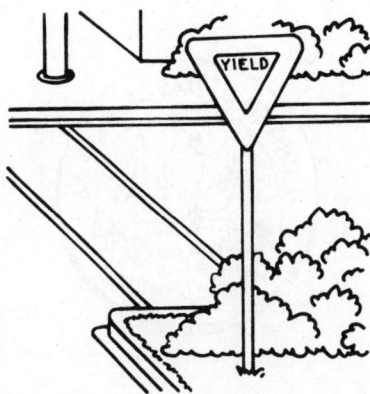
yield

yucca

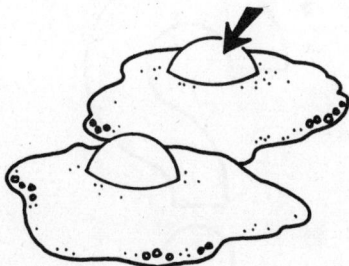
yolks

yawn

1. Yy   2. Yy   3. Yy

4. Yy   5. Yy   6. Yy

7. Yy   8. Yy   9. Yy

Aa Bb Cc Dd Ee Ff Gg Hh Ii Jj Kk Ll Mm Nn Oo Pp Qq Rr Ss Tt Uu Vv Ww Xx Yy Zz

quarter

quail

quart

queen

question

quilt

1. Qq   2. Qq   3. Qq

4. Qq   5. Qq   6. Qq

7. Qq   8. Qq   9. Qq

Aa Bb Cc Dd Ee Ff Gg Hh Ii
Jj Kk Ll Mm Nn Oo Pp Qq Rr
Ss Tt Uu Vv Ww ⟦Xx⟧ Yy Zz

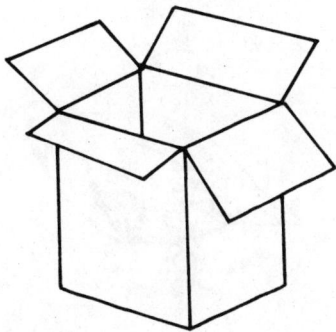

box

six

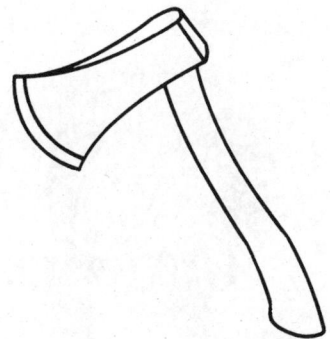

ax

fox

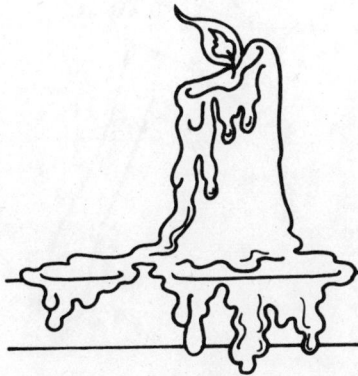

wax

ox

1. Xx   2. Xx   3. Xx

4. Xx   5. Xx   6. Xx

7. Xx   8. Xx   9. Xx

_____ard

_____uarter

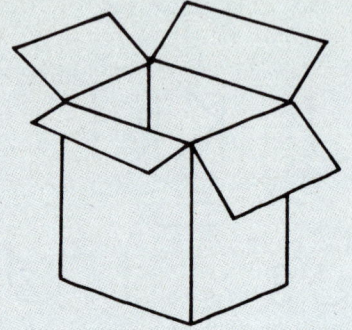

bo_____

_____arn

si_____

_____uail

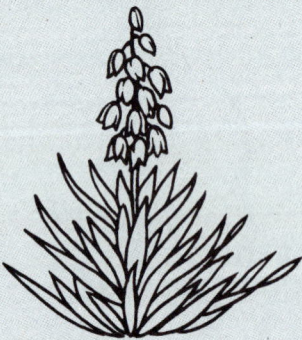

_____ucca

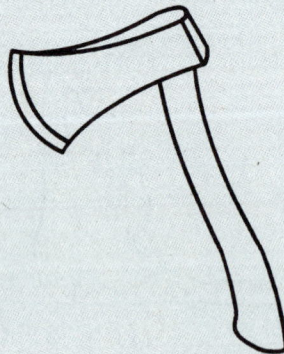

a_____

_____uart

1. _____

2. _____

3. _____

4. _____

5. _____

6. _____

7. _____

8. _____

9. _____

1. _____   2. _____   3. _____

4. _____   5. _____   6. _____

7. _____   8. _____   9. _____

10. _____   11. _____   12. _____

____oney

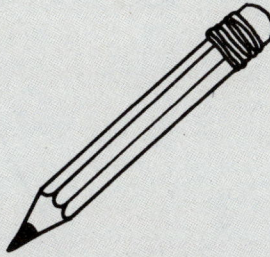

____encil

____ire

____ug

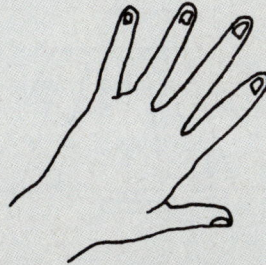

____and

____og

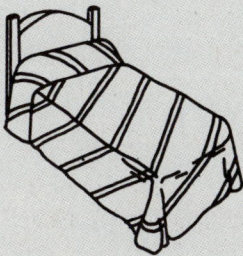

____ed

____itten

____ose

Aa Bb Cc Dd Ee Ff Gg Hh Ii
Jj Kk Ll Mm Nn Oo Pp Qq Rr
Ss Tt Uu Vv Ww Xx Yy Zz

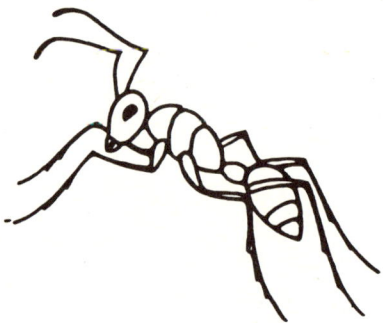

ant

apple

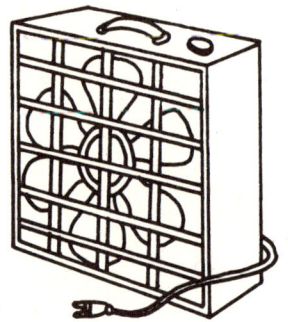

fan

man

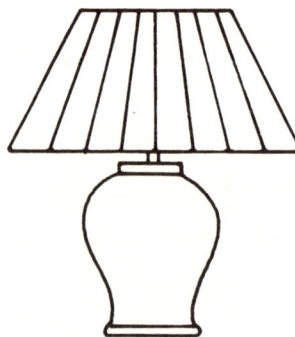

lamp

hat

1. Aa   2. Aa   3. Aa

4. Aa   5. Aa   6. Aa

7. Aa   8. Aa   9. Aa

Aa Bb Cc Dd Ee Ff Gg Hh Ii Jj Kk Ll Mm Nn Oo Pp Qq Rr Ss Tt Uu Vv Ww Xx Yy Zz

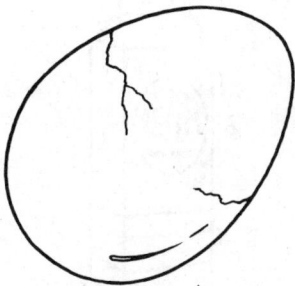

egg

bench

web

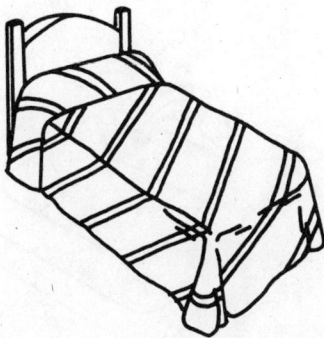

bed

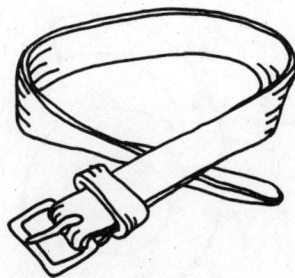

belt

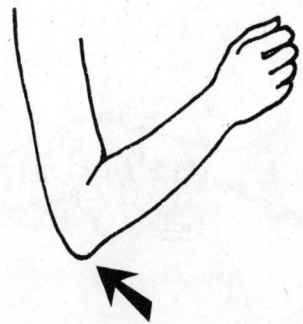

elbow

1. Ee   2. Ee   3. Ee

4. Ee   5. Ee   6. Ee

7. Ee   8. Ee   9. Ee

Aa Bb Cc Dd Ee Ff Gg Hh Ii
Jj Kk Ll Mm Nn Oo Pp Qq Rr
Ss Tt Uu Vv Ww Xx Yy Zz

ink

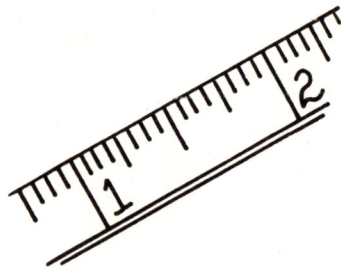

inch

milk

fish

six

sink

1. Ii   2. Ii   3. Ii

4. Ii   5. Ii   6. Ii

7. Ii   8. Ii   9. Ii

Aa Bb Cc Dd Ee Ff Gg Hh Ii
Jj Kk Ll Mm Nn Oo Pp Qq Rr
Ss Tt Uu Vv Ww Xx Yy Zz

octopus

pot

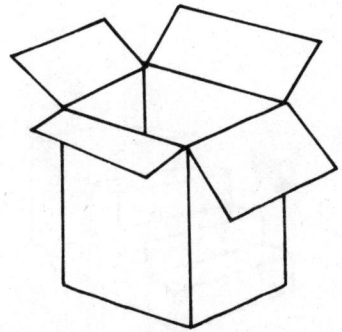

box

rock

mop

fox

1. Oo   2. Oo   3. Oo

4. Oo   5. Oo   6. Oo

7. Oo   8. Oo   9. Oo

Aa Bb Cc Dd Ee Ff Gg Hh Ii
Jj Kk Ll Mm Nn Oo Pp Qq Rr
Ss Tt **Uu** Vv Ww Xx Yy Zz

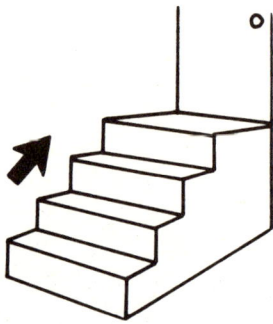

up

duck

cup

bus

rug

sun

1. Uu   2. Uu   3. Uu

4. Uu   5. Uu   6. Uu

7. Uu   8. Uu   9. Uu

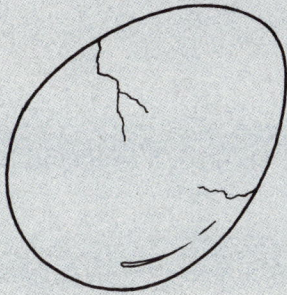

__e__gg

m____lk

c____p

f____x

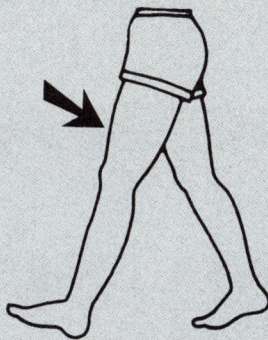

l____g

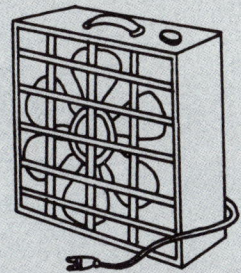

f____n

b____s

____nk

h____t

1. ____Oo____   2. _____   3. _____

4. _____   5. _____   6. _____

7. _____   8. _____   9. _____

1. Aa   2. Ii   3. Oo

4. Oo   5. Aa   6. Ee

7. Ee   8. Uu   9. Ii

1. _____   2. _____   3. _____

4. _____   5. _____   6. _____

7. _____   8. _____   9. _____

1.

w_____tch

2.

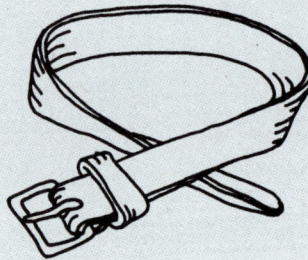

b_____lt

3.

b_____s

4.

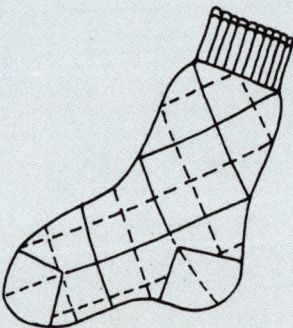

s_____ck

5.

r_____ng

6.

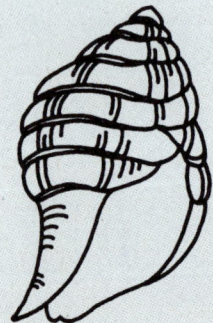

sh_____ll

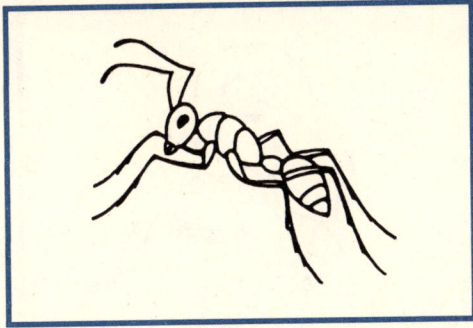

ant

ape

1.

(ant)   ape

2.

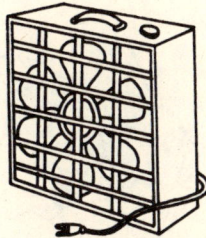

ant   ape

3.

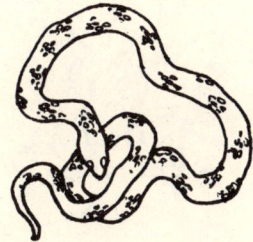

ant   ape

4.

ant   ape

5.

ant   ape

6.

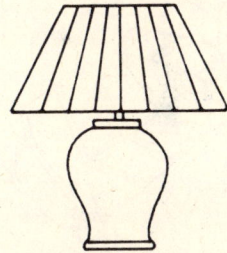

ant   ape

7.

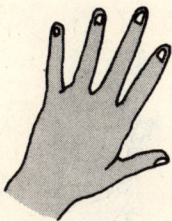

ant   ape

8.

ant   ape

9.

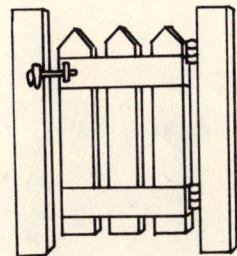

ant   ape

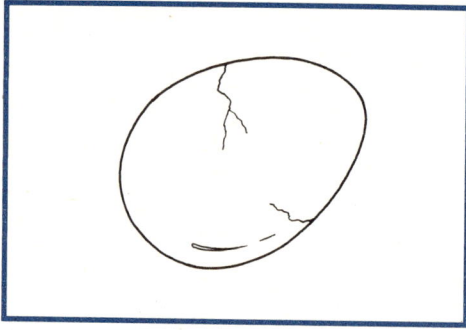

egg

eat

1.

egg   eat

2.

egg   eat

3.

egg   eat

4.

egg   eat

5.

egg   eat

6.

egg   eat

7.

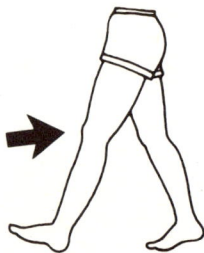

egg   eat

8.

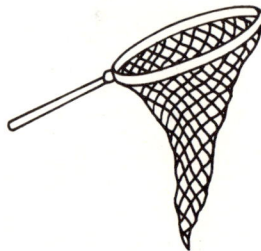

egg   eat

9.

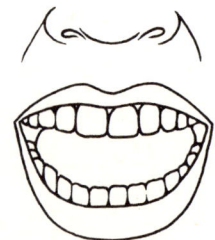

egg   eat

ink

ice

1.

ink   ice

2.

ink   ice

3.

ink   ice

4.

ink   ice

5.

ink   ice

6.

ink   ice

7.

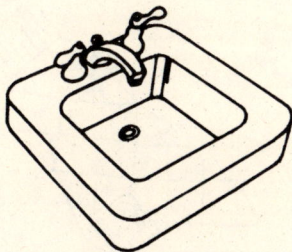

ink   ice

8.

ink   ice

9.

ink   ice

octopus

ocean

1.

octopus   ocean

2.

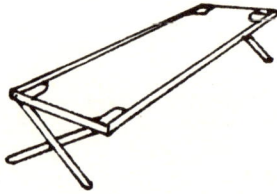

octopus   ocean

3.

octopus   ocean

4.

octopus   ocean

5.

octopus   ocean

6.

octopus   ocean

7.

octopus   ocean

8.

octopus   ocean

9.

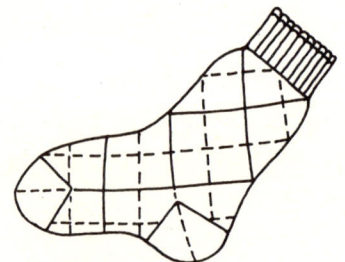

octopus   ocean

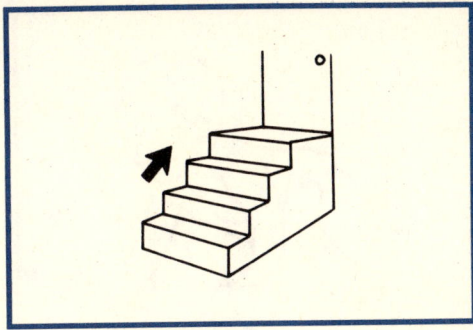

up

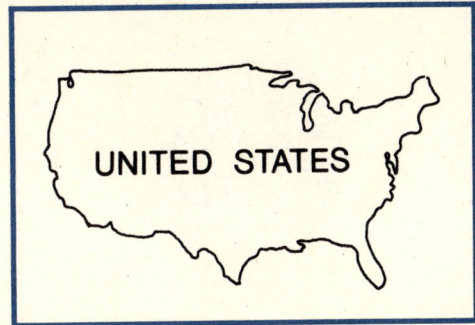

United States

1.

up   United States

2.

up   United States

3.

up   United States

4.

up   United States

5.

up   United States

6.

up   United States

7.

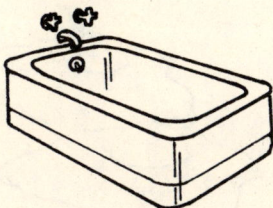

up   United States

8.

up   United States

9.

up   United States

yarn

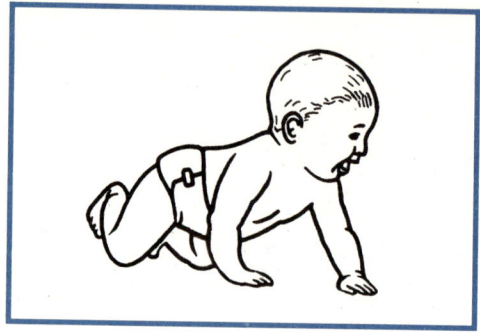

baby

1.

yarn   baby

2.

yarn   baby

3.

yarn   baby

4.

KENTUCKY

yarn   baby

5.

IN GOD WE TRUST

LIBERTY

1973

yarn   baby

6.

yarn   baby

7.

YIELD

yarn   baby

8.

NEW
JERSEY

yarn   baby

9.

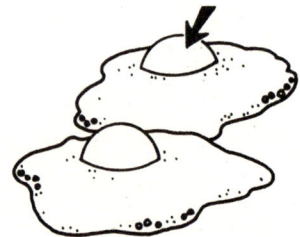

yarn   baby

cup

cereal

1.

cup   cereal

2.

cup   cereal

3.

cup   cereal

4.

cup   cereal

5.

cup   cereal

6.

cup   cereal

7.

cup   cereal

8.
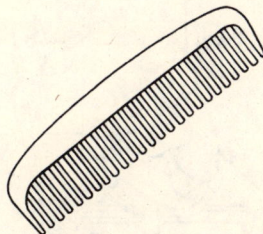
cup   cereal

9.

cup   cereal

guitar

giraffe

1.

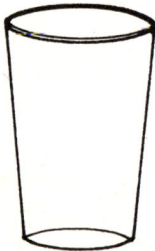

guitar   giraffe

2.

guitar   giraffe

3.

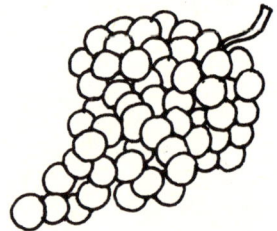

guitar   giraffe

4.

guitar   giraffe

5.

guitar   giraffe

6.

guitar   giraffe

7.

guitar   giraffe

8.

guitar   giraffe

9.

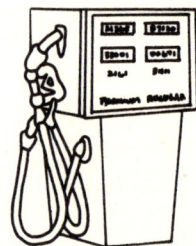

guitar   giraffe

cup   cereal

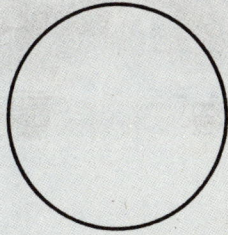

cup   cereal

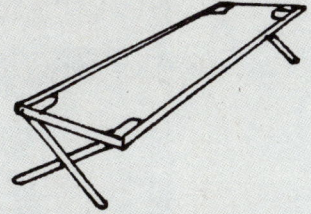

cup   cereal

guitar   giraffe

guitar   giraffe

guitar   giraffe

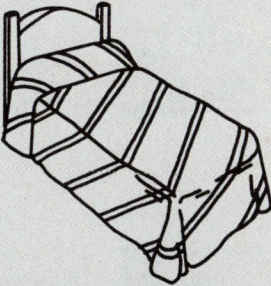

egg   eat

egg   eat

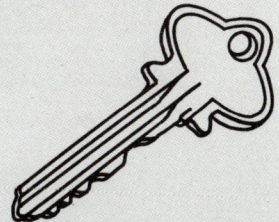

egg   eat

octopus   ocean

octopus   ocean

octopus   ocean

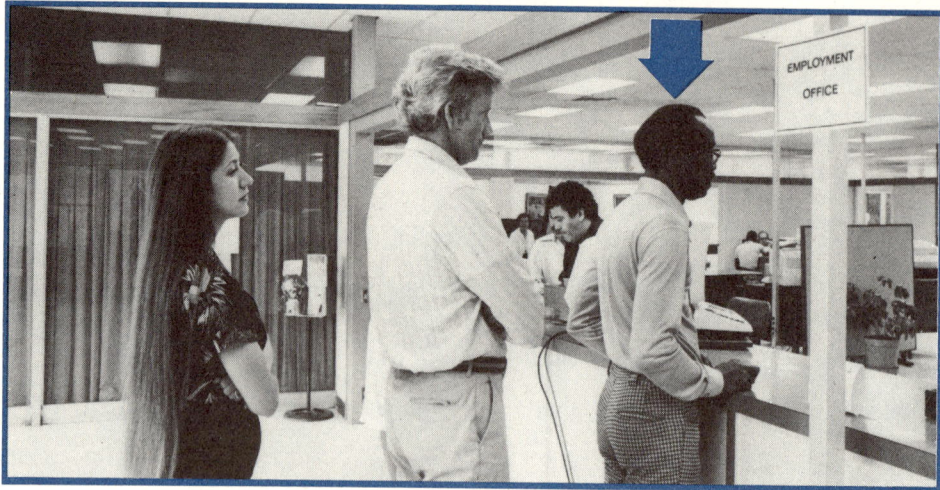

Beginning

End

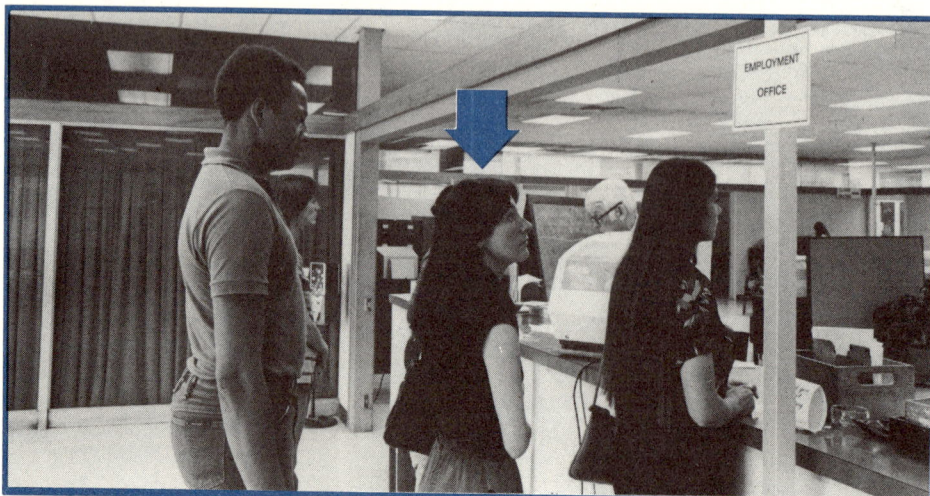

Middle

CAT

C is at the <u>beginning</u> of the word.

T is at the <u>end</u> of the word.

A is in the <u>middle</u> of the word.

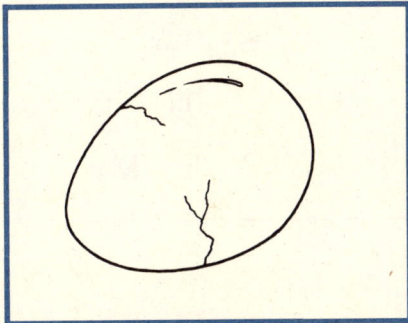

EGG

E is at the _____ of the word.

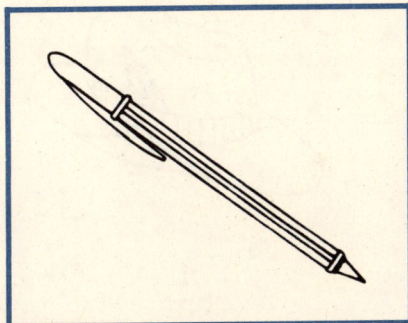

TABLE

E is at the _____ of the word.

PEN

E is in the _____ of the word.

B = Beginning   E = End   M = Middle

coat

(B) E M

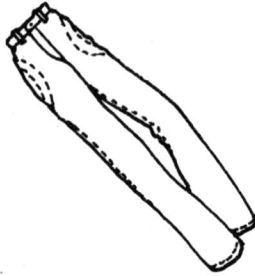

pants

B E M

shirt

B E M

dr__ess

B E M

suit

B E M

cap

B E M

shoes

B E M

sweater

B E M

hat

B E M

A a

apple

| am Ⓑ E M | Rita B E M |
| bat B E M | that B E M |

E e

elephant

| bed B E M | rice B E M |
| end B E M | tea B E M |

I i

ink

| milk B E M | Is B E M |
| king B E M | inch B E M |

O o

fox

| go B E M | hot B E M |
| clock B E M | on B E M |

U u

umbrella

| us B E M | Utah B E M |
| tub B E M | flu B E M |

B E M

B E M

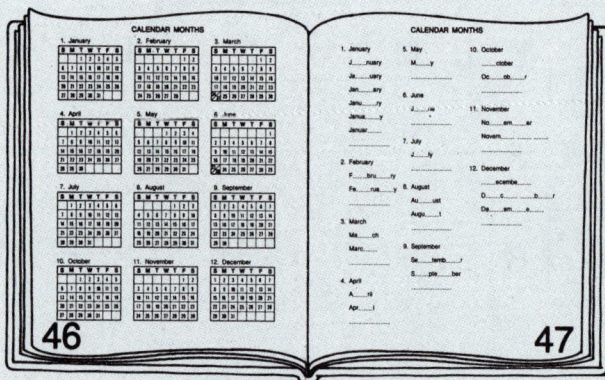

B E M

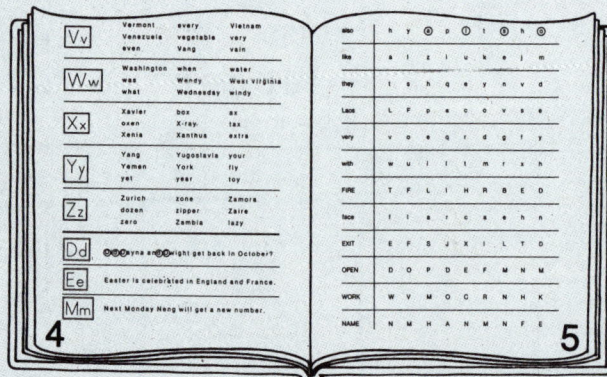

B E M

1. | <u>a</u>nswer | | airplan<u>e</u> | | b<u>i</u>ll

B E M   B E M   B E M

2. | c<u>a</u>r | | b<u>o</u>y | | coff<u>e</u>e

B E M   B E M   B E M

3. | j<u>u</u>g | | Lis<u>a</u> | | <u>u</u>se

B E M   B E M   B E M

B

1.

house   mouse

B

2.

cat   bat

E

3.

bus   rug

E

4.

road   top

M

5.

cup   cap

M

6.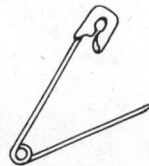

pin   pen

E

7.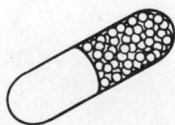

pig   pill

M

8.

beet   boat

1. (f)  f

2. r  r

3. k 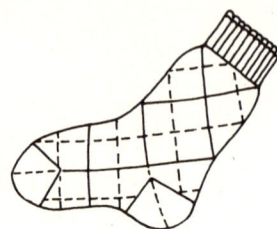 k

4. l  l

5. p  p

6. t  t

7. n  n

8. j  j

9. v  v

1.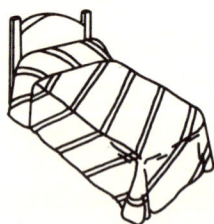

_____ed

2.

cu_____

3.

_____ire

4.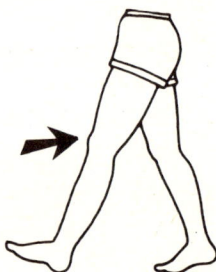

le_____

5.

_____ilk

6.

_____ey

56

1.

B

_____

2.

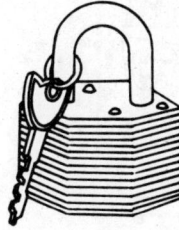 

_____

1.

E

_____

2.

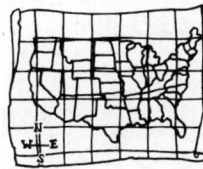 

_____

1.

M

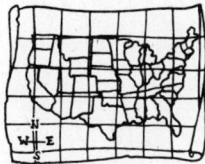 

_____

2.

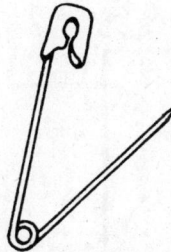 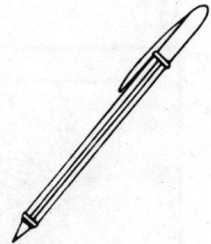

_____

B		**E**		**M**	
1. a	e	1. f	p	1. a	e
2. b	d	2. t	b	2. o	a
3. r	l	3. f	v	3. u	i
4. w	v	4. m	n	4. i	e

1.  corn (bat) (ball) table

2. 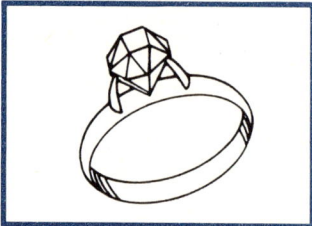 road load look bill

3. 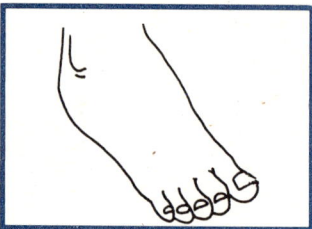 put fill book pipe

1.  off go sit till

2.  more back woman born

3. 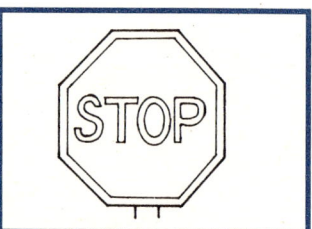 PUSH BUS PUP PULL

M

1.  in   this   moon   wake

2.  tent   pants   road   lamp

3.  bill   book   neck   key

4. 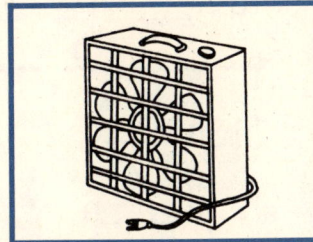 top   lid   that   film

B	**E**	**M**
1. r l t	1. p f z	1. a e u
2. w v	2. t d	2. a e
3. j y	3. s z	3. i e
4. i e	4. e v	4. o u
5. _____	5. _____	5. _____

B	E	M
B	**E**	**M**
1. ____ill	1. co____	1. n____t
2. ____ill	2. co____	2. n____t
3. ____ill	3. co____	3. n____t
4. ____ill	4. co____	
5. ____ill	5. co____	4. p____t
6. ____ill		5. p____t
7. ____ill	6. ca____	6. p____t
8. ____ill	7. ca____	7. p____t
9. ____ill	8. ca____	
10. ____ill	9. ca____	8. f____n
	10. ca____	9. f____n
11. ____am	11. ca____	10. f____n
12. ____am		
13. ____am	12. si____	11. b____n
14. ____am	13. si____	12. b____n
15. ____am	14. si____	13. b____n
	15. si____	
16. ____in	16. si____	
17. ____in		
18. ____in		
19. ____in		
20. ____in		

B

1. cot	(dog)	call	car
2. pin	put	sat	pet
3. zip	zoo	zero	sit
4. wife	wine	vine	want
5. tame	time	tip	lame
6. line	band	limb	lady

E

1. cut	fat	wig	wet
2. if	off	leaf	pup
3. desk	list	risk	kick
4. bad	bet	sod	red
5. wag	dig	plug	wax
6. bend	had	lab	mad

M

1. van	fan	bad	bud
2. hit	big	son	rib
3. hop	run	pop	mom
4. bug	hug	cut	cat
5. beg	leg	log	bet
6. cane	came	rain	vine

B

1. ____ood	f p d
2. ____ar	r w v
3. ____am	j y h
4. ____uice	j z
5. ____ife	w v
6. ____ad	h j
7. ____and	b c
8. ____am	w j
9. ____oy	t d
10. ____oad	_____

E

1. Mo____	m n g
2. funn____	v y g
3. lam____	f p t
4. bu____	s z
5. ra____	t d
6. ro____	b g
7. ba____	g j
8. co____	w v
9. jo____	z y
10. ba____	_____

M

1. s____ck	o e y
2. p____ll	i e a
3. m____ss	i e o
4. f____zz	i u
5. t____n	i a
6. c____n	e a
7. n____w	u e
8. d____me	i y
9. st____p	o a
10. c____t	_____

B E M

1. t____b	_____
2. ____ip	_____
3. hear____	_____
4. ____ine	_____
5. laz____	_____
6. m____ce	_____
7. d____ne	_____
8. craz____	_____
9. h____nd	_____
10. bea____	_____

1.

B 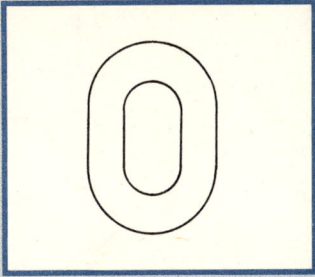   sand   zoo   bus   jar

2.

E    red   pull   zip   if

3.

M    bus   sin   us   call

B	E	M
1. a e	1. p f	1. o u
2. r l	2. t d	2. e i
3. _____ire	3. ga_____	3. fe_____t
4. _____ear	4. fro_____	4. h_____ll
5. _____ar	5. lea_____	5. v_____te
6. _____ame	6. stree_____	6. ph_____ne
7. _____ddress	7. cit_____	7. y_____s

B	E	M
1. _____et	1. bi_____	1. h_____m
2. _____et	2. bi_____	2. h_____m
3. _____et	3. bi_____	3. h_____m
4. _____et	4. bi_____	
5. _____et	5. bi_____	
6. _____et		

B

1. fox	feel	(pet)	food
2. jam	yet	you	yours
3. letter	loan	leave	bill
4. day	boat	bay	boy

E

1. hop	zip	zap	happy
2. mud	sad	sun	kid
3. pet	let	get	nod
4. cab	bad	lab	jab

M

1. bag	red	get	pen
2. Mom	hot	put	top
3. ten	time	hide	gin
4. gun	mule	cube	cape

DAYS OF THE WEEK

JUNE

1	2	3	4	5	6	7
Sunday	Monday	Tuesday	Wednesday	Thursday	Friday	Saturday
			1	2	3	4
5	6	7	8	9	10	11
12	13	14	15	16	17	18
19	20	21	22	23	24	25
26	27	28	29	30		

Sunday   Monday   Tuesday

Sunday _____ _____ _____

Wednesday   Thursday

_____ _____

Friday   Saturday

_____ _____

Monday ⌢ *Tuesday* _____ _____ ⌢ Tuesday

Thursday ⌢ _____ _____ ⌢ Wednesday

_____ ⌢ Saturday Friday ⌢ _____

Saturday ⌢ _____ Sunday ⌢ _____

DAYS OF THE WEEK

JUNE

S	M	T	W	T	F	S
Sun.	Mon.	Tues.	Wed.	Thurs.	Fri.	Sat.
			1	2	3	4
5	6	7	8	9	10	11
12	13	14	15	16	17	18
19	20	21	22	23	24	25
26	27	28	29	30		

Sunday

Monday

Tuesday

Wednesday

Thursday

Friday

Saturday

Thurs. _____

Sat. _____

Mon. _____

Fri. _____

Sun. _____*Sun.*_____

Wed. _____

Tues. _____

Sun. ⤻ _____*Mon.*_____

_____ ⤺ Sat.

Tues. ⤻ _____

_____ ⤺ Tues.

Wed. ⤻ _____

_____ ⤺ Fri.

Thurs. ⤻ _____

Fri. ⤻ _____

MONTHS OF THE YEAR

1. January

   J____nuary

   Ja____uary

   Jan____ary

   Janu____ry

   Janua____y

   Januar____

   _____

2. February

   F____bru____ry

   Fe____rua____y

   _____

3. March

   Ma____ch

   Marc____

   _____

4. April

   A____ril

   Apr____l

   _____

5. May

   M____y

   _____

6. June

   J____ne

   _____

7. July

   J____ly

   _____

8. August

   Au____ust

   Augu____t

   _____

9. September

   Se____temb____r

   S____pte____ber

   _____

10. October

    ____ctober

    Oc____ob____r

    _____

11. November

    No____em____er

    Novem____ ____ ____

    _____

12. December

    ____ecembe____

    D____c____ ____b____r

    De____em____e____

    _____

MONTHS OF THE YEAR

1. August is the (8th, 3rd) month of the year.

2. February is the (1st, 2nd) month of the year.

3. March is the (2nd, 3rd) month of the year.

4. December is the (2nd, 12th) month of the year.

5. July is the (11th, 7th) month of the year.

6. October is the (10th, 11th) month of the year.

7. June is the (6th, 9th) month of the year.

8. January is the (11th, 1st) month of the year.

9. April is the (4th, 7th) month of the year.

10. May is the (3rd, 5th) month of the year.

11. September is the (6th, 9th) month of the year.

12. November is the (10th, 11th) month of the year.

---

1. August 17 is on (Saturday, Sunday).

2. May 21 is on (Wednesday, Tuesday).

3. January 13 is on (Sunday, Monday).

4. October 17 is on (Tuesday, Thursday).

5. August 30 is on (Saturday, Friday).

6. February 6 is on (Tuesday, Wednesday).

7. December 25 is on (Wednesday, Thursday).

8. June 1 is on (Sunday, Saturday).

MONTHS OF THE YEAR

1. Jan. _____

S	M	T	W	T	F	S
		1	2	3	4	5
6	7	8	9	10	11	12
13	14	15	16	17	18	19
20	21	22	23	24	25	26
27	28	29	30	31		

2. Feb. _____

S	M	T	W	T	F	S
					1	2
3	4	5	6	7	8	9
10	11	12	13	14	15	16
17	18	19	20	21	22	23
24	25	26	27	28		

3. Mar. _____

S	M	T	W	T	F	S
					1	2
3	4	5	6	7	8	9
10	11	12	13	14	15	16
17	18	19	20	21	22	23
24/31	25	26	27	28	29	30

4. Apr. _____

S	M	T	W	T	F	S
	1	2	3	4	5	6
7	8	9	10	11	12	13
14	15	16	17	18	19	20
21	22	23	24	25	26	27
28	29	30				

5. May _____

S	M	T	W	T	F	S
			1	2	3	4
5	6	7	8	9	10	11
12	13	14	15	16	17	18
19	20	21	22	23	24	25
26	27	28	29	30	31	

6. June _____

S	M	T	W	T	F	S
						1
2	3	4	5	6	7	8
9	10	11	12	13	14	15
16	17	18	19	20	21	22
23/30	24	25	26	27	28	29

7. July _____

S	M	T	W	T	F	S
	1	2	3	4	5	6
7	8	9	10	11	12	13
14	15	16	17	18	19	20
21	22	23	24	25	26	27
28	29	30	31			

8. Aug. _____

S	M	T	W	T	F	S
				1	2	3
4	5	6	7	8	9	10
11	12	13	14	15	16	17
18	19	20	21	22	23	24
25	26	27	28	29	30	31

9. Sept. _____

S	M	T	W	T	F	S
1	2	3	4	5	6	7
8	9	10	11	12	13	14
15	16	17	18	19	20	21
22	23	24	25	26	27	28
29	30					

10. Oct. _____

S	M	T	W	T	F	S
		1	2	3	4	5
6	7	8	9	10	11	12
13	14	15	16	17	18	19
20	21	22	23	24	25	26
27	28	29	30	31		

11. Nov. _____

S	M	T	W	T	F	S
					1	2
3	4	5	6	7	8	9
10	11	12	13	14	15	16
17	18	19	20	21	22	23
24	25	26	27	28	29	30

12. Dec. _____

S	M	T	W	T	F	S
1	2	3	4	5	6	7
8	9	10	11	12	13	14
15	16	17	18	19	20	21
22	23	24	25	26	27	28
29	30	31				

MONTHS OF THE YEAR

1st	November	
2nd	June	
3rd	February	
4th	October	
5th	January	*January*
6th	May	
7th	September	
8th	December	
9th	March	
10th	August	
11th	April	
12th	July	

January	Apr.	
February	Aug.	
March	Oct.	
April	Dec.	
August	Sept.	
September	Jan.	
October	Mar.	
November	Feb.	
December	Nov.	

1st	February	Sept.
4th	November	Mar.
7th	January	Apr.
9th	September	Dec.
11th	April	July
12th	March	Feb.
3rd	December	Nov.
2nd	October	Jan.
10th	July	Oct.

Feb. ⌒ _____ *Mar.*

Mar. ⌒ _____

_____ ⌒ May

June ⌒ _____

_____ ⌒ Aug.

Oct. ⌒ _____

1st	Saturday	Sun.
4th	Sunday	Thurs.
5th	Wednesday	Sat.
7th	Thursday	Wed.

Mon. ⌒ _____

_____ ⌒ Tues.

Fri. ⌒ _____

_____ ⌒ Thurs.

Sun. ⌒ _____

Wed. ⌒ _____

_____ ⌒ Fri.

CALENDAR DATES

CALENDAR DATES

August 1991

Sunday	Monday	Tuesday	Wednesday	Thursday	Friday	Saturday
				1	②	3
4	5	6	⑦	8	9	10
11	12	13	14	⑮	16	17
⑱	19	20	21	22	23	24
25	26	㉗	28	29	30	㉛

August 2, 1991   8-2-91

_____   _____

_____   _____

December 1991

Sun.	Mon.	Tues.	Wed.	Thurs.	Fri.	Sat.
①	2	3	4	5	6	7
8	9	10	11	12	⑬	14
15	⑯	17	18	19	20	21
22	23	24	25	26	27	㉘
29	30	31				

December 1, 1991   12-1-91

_____   _____

_____   _____

Spouse

_____   _____
Name   Date of Birth

Children

1st _____   _____
Name   Date of Birth

2nd _____   _____
Name   Date of Birth

3rd _____   _____
Name   Date of Birth

4th _____   _____
Name   Date of Birth

5th _____   _____
Name   Date of Birth

6th _____   _____
Name   Date of Birth

TIME

1. What time is it?

_____

2. What time is it?

_____

3. What time is it?

_____

4. What time is it?

_____

5. What time is it?

_____

6. What time is it?

_____

TIME

1. What time is it?

2. What time is it?

3. What time is it?

4. What time is it?

5. What time is it?

6. What time is it?

7. What time is it?

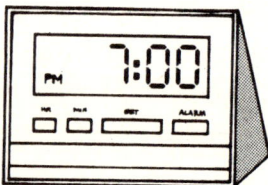

8. What time is it?

TIME

1. What time is it?

1:00

3 o'clock

5:45

2. What time is it?

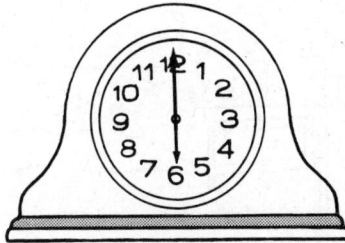

11:45

6 o'clock

5:00

3. What time is it?

2:15

11:30

11:00

4: Is it 4:00?

Yes, it is.

No, it isn't.

5. Is it 5:15?

Yes, it is.

No, it isn't.

6. Is it 10:45?

Yes, it is.

No, it isn't.

7. What time is it?

_____

8. What time is it?

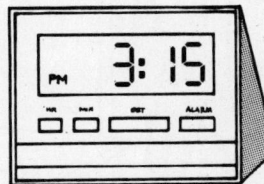 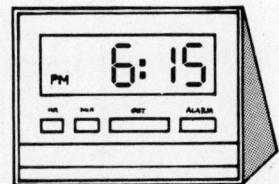

_____

TIME

6:45 A.M.

9:00 A.M.

2:30 P.M.

6:30 P.M.

10:30 P.M.

12:00 noon

12:00 midnight

TIME

1. Is it 5:15 P.M.?

Yes, it is.

No, it isn't.

2. Is it 7:45 A.M.?

Yes, it is.

No, it isn't.

3. Is it 12:15 P.M.?

Yes, it is.

No, it isn't.

4. Is it 8:30 P.M.?

Yes, it is.

No, it isn't.

5. Is it 11:30 A.M.?

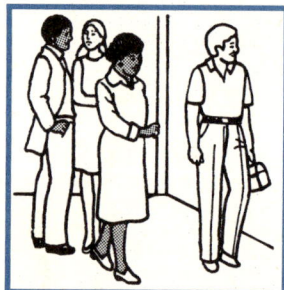 

Yes, it is.

No, it isn't.

6. Is it 5:30 A.M.?

Yes, it is.

No, it isn't.

TIME

1.

2:45 P.M.

12:00 noon

2.

7:30 A.M.

5:45 P.M.

10:30 P.M.

3.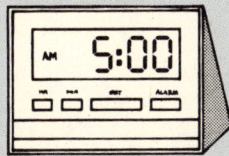

12:00 midnight

9:15 A.M.

4.

8:45 P.M.

5 o'clock A.M.

6:15 P.M.

5.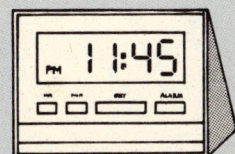

11:45 P.M.

CH

A a B b C c D d E e F f G g H h I i
J j K k L l M m N n O o P p Q q R r
S s T t U u V v W w X x Y y Z z

CH

chair

match

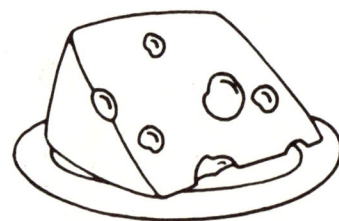

cheese

children

watch

sandwich

1. ch   2. ch   3. ch

4. ch   5. ch   6. ch

7. ch   8. ch   9. ch

82

SH

A a B b C c D d E e F f G g H h I i
J j K k L l M m N n O o P p Q q R r
S s T t U u V v W w X x Y y Z z

SH

sheep

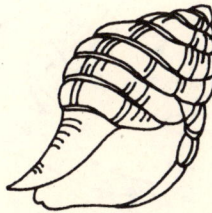

shell

fish

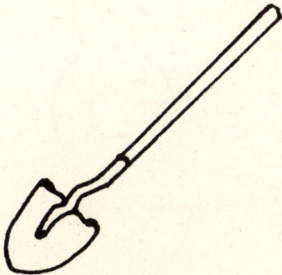

shovel

shoe

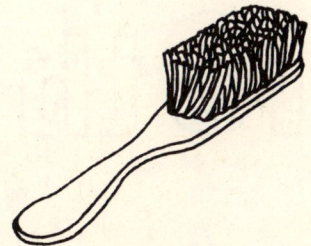

brush

1. sh   2. sh   3. sh

4. sh   5. sh   6. sh

7. sh   8. sh   9. sh

Aa Bb Cc Dd Ee Ff Gg Hh Ii
Jj Kk Ll Mm Nn Oo Pp Qq Rr
Ss Tt Uu Vv Ww Xx Yy Zz

TH

thumb

mouth

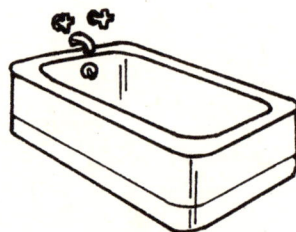

bathtub

10th

tenth

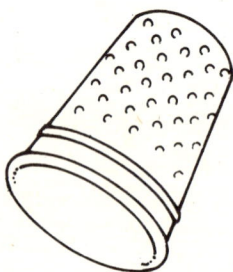

thimble

3

three

1. th
2. th
3. th
4. th
5. th
6. th
7. th
8. th
9. th

SH	S

ship

sip

1.

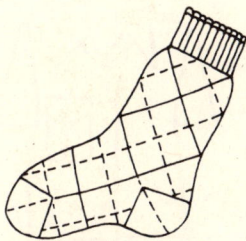

sh   s

2.

sh   s

3.

sh   s

4.

sh   s

5.

sh   s

6.

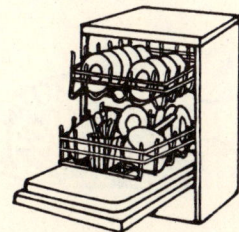

sh   s

7.

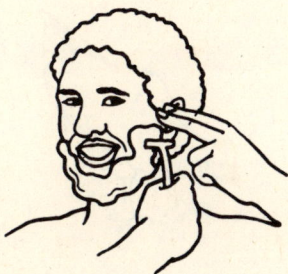

sh   s

8.

sh   s

9.

sh   s

SH

ships

CH

chips

1.

sh   ch

2.

sh   ch

3.

sh   ch

4.

sh   ch

5.

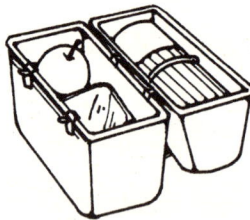

sh   ch

6.

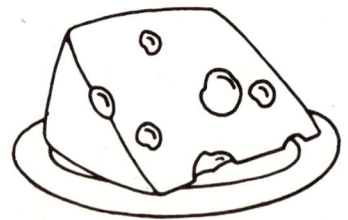

sh   ch

7.

sh   ch

8.

sh   ch

9.

sh   ch

T

tie

TH

thirty

1.

t   th

2.

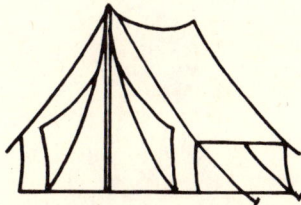

t   th

3.

t   th

4.

t   th

5.

t   th

6.

t   th

7.

t   th

8.

t   th

9.

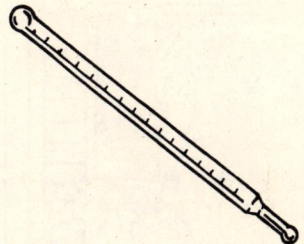

t   th

SH

shirt

TH

third

1.

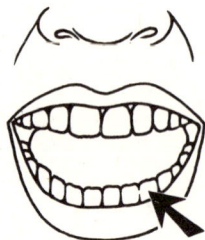

sh   th

2.

sh   th

3.

sh   th

4.

sh   th

5.

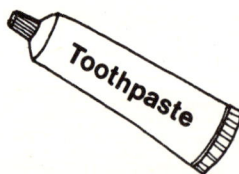

sh   th

6.

sh   th

7.

sh   th

8.

sh   th

9.

sh   th

S	TH
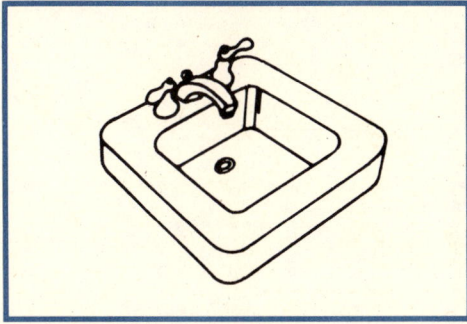	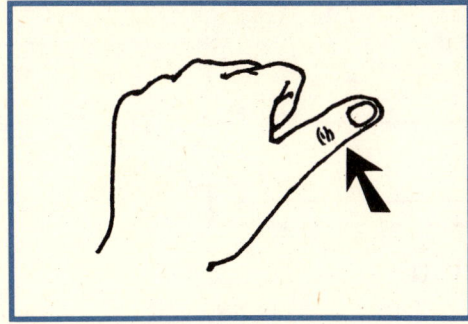
sink	thumb

1.
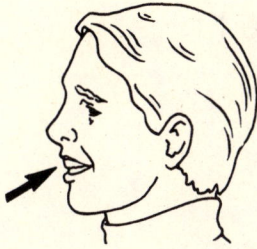
s   th

2.
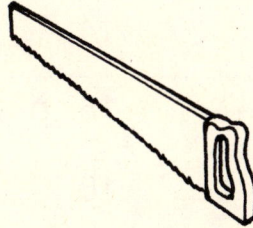
s   th

3.
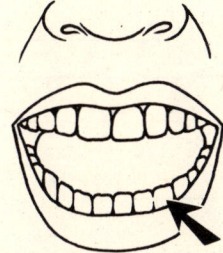
s   th

4.
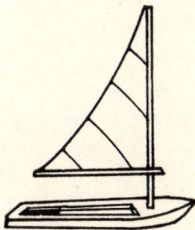
s   th

5.

s   th

6.

s   th

7.
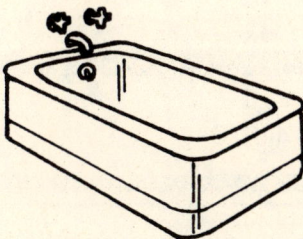
s   th

8.
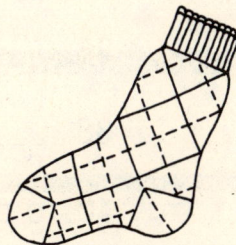
s   th

9.

s   th

89

ch   s   sh   t   th

1. _____ _____ e w   2. _____ _____ u t

3. _____ _____ o p   4. b u _____

5. m u _____ _____   6. _____ _____ y

7. c a _____ _____ e d   8. w i _____ _____

9. _____ a v e   10. _____ _____ a n k

11. s t a r _____   12. r e n _____

13. w i _____ _____   14. _____ _____ e l f

15. _____ _____ i n   16. p a _____ _____

17. _____ i c k   18. _____ e w

19. _____ e n   20. _____ _____ e m e

21. c r a _____ _____   22. o u _____ _____

23. _____ _____ i l d r e n 24. c o a _____

25. b o _____ _____   26. f i _____ _____

27. _____ _____ o w   28. h i _____

29. _____ u n   30. _____ _____ a i n

31. d e a _____ _____   32. _____ i m e

33. _____ _____ e e s e   34. _____ i n g

35. _____ _____ o e   36. _____ i l k

37. b a _____   38. _____ _____ i n e

39. _____ a l t   40. c a _____ _____

B
1. says   shop   shoot   shed
2. cheek   city   chop   check
3. thick   thought   tell   thing

E
1. with   bath   math   mash
2. March   trash   beach   inch
3. want   light   boot   cloth

1.

_____ _____ell

2.

_____ _____ree

3.

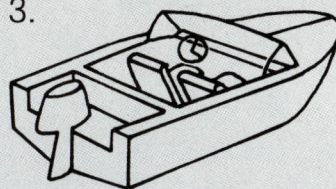

boa_____

4.

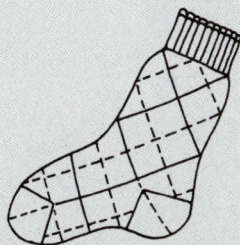

_____ock

5.

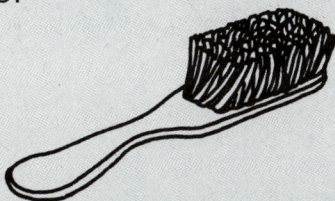

bru_____ _____

6.

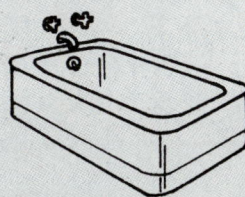

ba_____ _____tub

7.

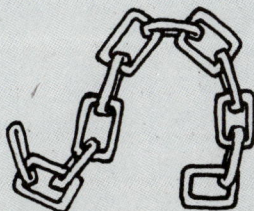

_____ _____ain

8.

bu_____

9.

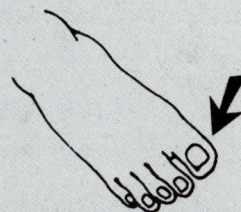

_____oe

SH	1. sh	2. sh	3. sh
CH	1. ch	2. ch	3. ch
TH	1. th	2. th	3. th
T	1. t	2. t	3. t
S	1. s	2. s	3. s

1.

sh   s

2.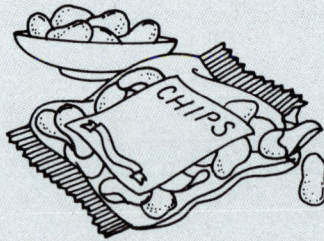

sh   ch

3.

t   th

4.
3rd

sh   th

5.
3

s   th

6.

sh   s

ch   s   sh   t   th

1. _____ _____ ank

2. _____ ime

3. ma _____ _____

4. fi _____ _____

5. _____ _____ ildren

6. _____ _____ eep

7. mu _____ _____

8. bu _____

9. si _____